**KU-507-152**

# CONTENTS

# ACKNOWLEDGEMENTS

I would like to thank everybody at HarperElement and LIVINGtv and all the people who have helped over the past 12 months.

# INTRODUCTION

> **'All houses wherein men have lived and died
> are haunted houses!'**
>
> Longfellow

Following the tremendous success of *Ghost Hunting with Derek Acorah*, I was inundated with requested to compile a book of locations throughout Scotland that are reputed to be haunted – and I was certainly spoiled for choice.

One of the most difficult things when deciding to go on an investigation into the paranormal is finding the right location. Hopefully *Haunted Scotland* will take the hard work out of this by suggesting some of the most haunted places in Scotland, divided into areas for ease of reference. No matter where you live or how little you are prepared to travel, there will always be somewhere worthy of a visit if you are on the hunt for a ghost or two.

While I have not yet been able to visit all the places covered in this book, I very much hope to investigate them in the future. Some of these sites may be slightly off the beaten track, but I'm sure all are worthy of the ghost hunter's attention.

When undertaking an investigation into the paranormal it is as well to remember that there are many different types of ghostly manifestation. First, there are the 'feelings' we all pick up from atmospheres. When entering premises, take care to note in which room or rooms you feel comfortable and in which you feel less at ease. Use your basic psychic senses – we all have them – to assist you in the first steps of your investigation by picking up on the residual energies left in a property by previous occupants. Obviously unless you are a trained medium you will not be able to experience specifics, but you should be able to identify areas where you feel there is more likelihood of paranormal activity. As you take an initial walk around the location, make notes on where you feel would be the most interesting sections to concentrate your investigation.

Of course not all 'hauntings' are the result of spirit presence. There are a variety of reports where people have described ghosts appearing at the same time on the same date of a year. These are known as 'anniversary' ghosts. If you are intending visiting a location alleged to have an anniversary ghost, please go along on the relevant day, as if you do not, you may well be disappointed.

There are also lots of grey ladies, blue ladies and occasionally a green lady or two haunting Scotland. Sites reporting this type of ghost are always well worth a visit as, although you may not be able to define the clothing or features of the 'lady' concerned, sightings are usually quite regular and so you are less likely to be disappointed in your quest.

Then there are the ghosts who walk through walls and disappear in the most unusual circumstances into fireplaces and the like. This happens because a spirit person visiting a former residence does not recognize any changes that have been made to the building – they perceive their former home or workplace as it was when they inhabited the mortal world. So where there was once a doorway, a door will still exist for them and they will continue to use it, thus giving the appearance of disappearing through a wall.

There are also earthbound spirits, i.e. spirits of people who have not moved on from this physical world, and the spirits of people who return in visitation to their old homes or places of work. If they wish, they may allow you to glimpse them. This may manifest itself in a number of ways. You may catch a slight movement out of the corner of your eye as you move around a place, you may see a shadow moving quickly from one part of a room to another or you may see spirit lights – bright lights flashing for a brief moment. All are signs that you are not alone.

The first thing to remember when conducting an investigation is that there are many ways in which the residents of that world beyond make their presence known to us. They may cause items to move, they may make all kinds of noises, they may brush past you or draw close to you, causing the atmosphere to chill considerably. What the investigator then has to do is confirm whether in fact there is spirit activity around or whether there is a logical and more worldly explanation for the movement of objects, the noises or the drop (or in some cases rise) in temperature. The use of a thermometer – and I would recommend the digital variety – will enable you to pinpoint temperature changes to within a degree.

Always make sure that when a noticeable temperature drop takes place you look for open windows or doors, open fireplaces or even loosely fitted window panes. All too often a draught may give rise to much excitement, only for that excitement to be dampened by the discovery that somebody has forgotten to close a door. If, after ensuring that all possible logical explanations have been dismissed, draughts are still felt moving around a room, it is more than likely that there is spirit presence there.

Parapsychologists use electromagnetic field meters to measure fluctuations in energy in an attempt to establish whether in fact there are paranormal events taking place, but I have found that EMF meters are not always capable of delivering an accurate indication of spirit presence.

The source of noises must also be examined before they can be attributed to a ghostly presence. Ensure that nobody is moving around or speaking in an adjoining room. Check to see that the noises are not emanating from the exterior of the building, i.e. cars, animals or passers-by.

Further interest can be added to an investigation by the use of audio recording equipment. Examples of electronic voice phenomenon have been widely reported in the press and you just may be fortunate enough to capture the voices of spirit entities on tape.

Another 'must have' on an investigation is camera equipment. A video recording of your experiences is a marvellous addition to your archives, but at the very least a camera of sorts should be taken along. This may enable you to capture different examples of phenomena such as orbs or traces of ectoplasm. It matters not whether the camera is of the digital or flash variety. Point it into the darkest recesses of a room at night and very often you will find that you have managed to photograph some type of paranormal phenomena.

If you are intending to hold a séance at the location it may be a good idea to place a lighted candle in the centre of the table. The flickering of the flame could indicate the movement through the atmosphere of a spirit being, but please do be careful and do not leave the candle unattended. Most importantly when holding a séance, do ask for protection from your guides and door-keepers in the world of spirit. Ask them to guard you and ensure that only the highest and the best spirit connection is made. After completing a séance, it is also important to close the circle down by sending whichever spirit people chose to call back to the light.

Apart from the above, the only other item which you have to take along to an investigation is your common sense. Do make sure that you respect the property of others. Do take along torches and spare batteries if you are visiting a location where there is no electricity connected and do wear suitable clothing and footwear.

With *Haunted Scotland* guiding your footsteps around haunted locations in Scotland you will have many, many hours of enjoyment to look forward to.

Good luck!

# WHAT IS A GHOST?

The word 'ghost' conjures up the image of a wispy wraith-like figure floating along the corridors of ancient buildings, lonely derelict monasteries or sites where historical events have taken place. In fact it is a generic word used to encompass paranormal sightings whenever they may occur. Ghosts can be ladies or gentlemen. They can be headless horsemen, tramps and crones or sprightly children. They can be dressed in modern garb. They are varied and innumerable and appear from all stages of the history of our world.

But what are ghosts? Simply, they are memories! Photographs in time! They are the result of the energy left in the fabric of a place or a building by the people who have lived, worked and died there. Today we are all imbuing the fabric of our homes and workplaces with *our* residual energies. In time to come mediums of the future will be picking up these energies and relating details of *our* lives to the people who are interested enough to listen. It will be possible for the actions of today to be picked up mediumistically by the sensitives of the future. Our daily lives leave an unseen and unwritten record in the fabric of the buildings we inhabit.

It follows of course that the more emotional the events in people's lives are, the stronger the energy they leave behind. A sensitive may pick up on the mundane day-to-day items but should something of great importance occur, whether it be great happiness or deep sadness, then the energies will be so much stronger and they will more readily tune into those energies.

This is rather well demonstrated by anniversary ghosts – those apparitions that appear at the same time on the same date in any given year. Usually they recall a tragic and untimely loss of life. Rarely do anniversary ghosts recall memories of great joy.

## What is a Spirit?

A spirit is a soul. Our spirit is the part of us that lives on for ever and is eternal. Once we have shed the physical garb and passed on through what is termed 'death', we progress into the world beyond, returning to the home from whence we came. Spirit people are as alive as you and I. They are merely people who live on a faster vibration as they are not weighed down by either the physical body or the cares that plague us during our lifetime here on Earth.

It is the spirit people with whom a medium such as I connects through either clairvoyance (clear seeing) or clairaudience (clear hearing). As well as communicating directly with a medium, spirit people may also choose to communicate through that medium's spirit guide, who will then act as an intermediary, passing on messages from the people in the world beyond to their loved ones who still live in this world.

You may have heard the term 'crises ghosts'. These are not in fact ghosts but a phenomenon that occurs when at the emotionally charged moment of death the spirit projects itself into the consciousness of the person or persons who were closest to it during its lifetime here on Earth. There have been many documented occasions when people have seen a member of their family appear before them, only for them to disappear just as quickly. They have later learned of the passing to spirit of that loved one at the precise moment of their experience.

The people in the spirit world are not burdened with timetables and do not have to cope with the rigors of travel. They can be where they want when they want. They can drop into their old home to see how their family are doing or can travel to any part of the world they choose to. Just because you go on holiday or move to another part of the globe it does not mean that your family in spirit do not travel with you if they wish to. The only difference is that they don't have to find the price of a ticket!

When a medium takes part in a paranormal investigation they will, through their sensitivity to the spirit world, pick up the presence of a spirit person, but it is not beyond the realms of possibility for anyone to see a spirit if that spirit person wishes them to do so. The people from the spirit world move on a much faster vibration than we do, but by slowing down they can become visible to us all. I liken it to watching the propeller of an aeroplane. When it is static or slow moving it is clear to everyone that what is there is a very solid piece of metal. Once the engine gains momentum, the propeller vanishes from sight and all we see is a blur. We know that the propeller is there, but we just can't see it. So it is with the spirit world. Spirits only become visible to us when they choose to slow down their vibrations.

## Psychic Breezes

During paranormal investigations the participants may become aware of areas of cool moving air in certain rooms. I call these 'psychic breezes' and they are caused by the movement of a spirit person around that particular room.

If a séance is held in a room where paranormal activity is recorded to have taken place, it is not unusual for the sitters to experience a feeling of coldness passing over their knees and hands as they sit generating energy in order to attract spirit presence.

In extreme cases, if an investigator is walking around an area which also contains a spirit presence, that investigator may well experience feelings of dizziness and slight nausea, or even an overwhelming flood of emotion, as they walk through the energy field of that spirit presence.

## Cold Spots and Hot Spots

These two terms are commonly heard during paranormal investigations, but what do they mean? I know that parapsychologists have their own interpretation, but how they arrive at their explanations I really don't know, as they certainly don't communicate with the spirit world and indeed, in some cases, deny its very existence.

From my understanding of what I have been told by my spirit guide Sam, a cold spot is a portal or vortex, a spiritual doorway which facilitates the entry and exit of visiting spirit people into and out of our earthly atmosphere. These cold spots do not move but remain in the same area of a building. They are not to be confused with the coolness of psychic breezes, which come and go with the movement of a spirit entity.

Hot spots are the energy of a grounded spirit, i.e. a spirit person who has chosen for whatever reason to remain close to our earthly atmosphere. These spirit people remain in the surroundings that were familiar to them in their earthly life. Unlike cold spots, which remain static, hot spots move from place to place with the movement of that spirit person. The heat is caused by the energy of the grounded spirit.

# PREPARATION

Preparation is essential for a successful ghost hunt, both to gain satisfactory evidence of any spirit activity and to rule out any other explanations. What will you need?

## Equipment

As a spirit medium, I both see and hear spirit naturally. I am able to pick up events that have taken place in a building from the atmosphere there. I like to think of such events as 'photographs in time', but they are more commonly known as residual energies, emotions from times gone by that linger in the fabric of a place.

Although many paranormal groups turn to mediums for assistance in their investigations, investigators will also need to include items of a more worldly nature in their kitbags to give tangible proof of spirit activity.

### A Torch

One obvious item is a torch. Take a supply of replacement batteries too – mischievous spirit presences like nothing better than to drain battery power and a hapless investigator who has forgotten to pack extra batteries could well end up fumbling around in the dark.

## Notebooks and Pens

Notebooks and pens will enable you to record details of events as they occur. The worst thing to do is to rely on memory, as after a long night's investigation recall can be blurred, especially if there have been many exciting incidents.

It is also a good idea to make a rough sketch of the location before commencing an investigation, numbering rooms for ease of reference.

Plain white paper and pencils are also a necessity so that an item or 'trigger object' can be placed on the paper and its outline traced. Any subsequent movement of the object can then easily be detected. Wooden crosses of a suitable size seem to be popular as trigger objects, though any item which has an easily traceable outline may be used.

## Cotton and Tape

It may be necessary to seal off certain rooms whilst tests are conducted. As security is not the issue here, simple black cotton and adhesive tape may be used.

A sealed room is the ideal location for a trigger object or for strategically placed cameras that will record any activity taking place.

## Candles

Household candles should also be included in the kit, as the flickering of their flames may reveal a spirit presence. Checks should be made prior to starting the investigation to ensure that there are no draughts which could cast doubt over the cause of a flickering flame. Of course lit candles must never be left unattended purely from a safety point of view.

## Flour

Prior to the investigation a raid on the kitchen cupboard should be made to acquire a bag of ordinary flour. When sprinkled over the floor this will reveal any footprints – or handprints, if sprinkled on a tabletop. A small soft brush should be used to distribute the flour over the desired area. Care should always be taken when investigating a property owned by another person and it may well be a good idea to spread the flour over sheets of old newspaper.

## Walkie-Talkies

Walkie-talkies or two-way radios are a good way for investigators to keep in touch with one another during an investigation. If you are contemplating splitting up into groups, or even going off individually whilst investigating a location, it is always a good idea to be able to contact your fellow investigators.

## A Thermometer

A thermometer is a must in order to detect fluctuations in the temperature of a room. I have seen large greenhouse-type thermometers used, but of course the serious ghost hunter will invest in a digital thermometer which gives the exact temperature on an 'easy to read' digital display.

## An EMF Meter

An electro-magnetic field or EMF meter is worth acquiring. These measure fluctuations in electromagnetic energy. Parapsychologists and paranormal investigators are of the general opinion that spirits cause such fluctuations.

When investigating a property using an EMF meter, all sources of electricity, i.e. cabling, and all electrical devices must be carefully noted, as such items also generate electro-magnetic fields. Any fluctuations displayed on the EMF meter should then be checked against the location of the electrical wiring. Once all such electricity sources have been established, anything registering over 2.5 milligauss on the EMF meter indicates a possible ghostly presence. I have found, however, that EMF meters are not always capable of delivering an accurate indication of a spirit presence.

## Pendulums and Dowsing Rods

Some ghost hunters favour the use of dowsing rods and pendulums. It is alleged that both devices can pick up the electro-magnetic energy field of a ghost.

Dowsing has been in use for many years. In ancient times, a 'Y'-shaped stick would be used to trace underground water sources. Today people tend to use a pair of specially prepared dowsing rods made of thick wire. Each rod is a basic 'L' shape but with a shorter foot and a longer upright. A rod is taken in each hand, with the shorter length held firmly in each fist and the longer end sticking straight out in front. Upon reaching an area of psychic activity, the rods will begin to swing wildly and cross over each other. Before attributing a dowsing rod reaction to paranormal activity, however, checks should be made to ensure there are no underground streams or other sources of water in the area.

It is said that most paranormal activity takes place in areas where many ley lines are present or at the junction of ley lines, so if investigators are aware of the location of these lines, they will have a clearer idea of where to commence their dowsing. To discover where these lines run, initially investigators would have to make enquiries of people at the locations or conduct prior research. They could of course spend many long hours walking backwards and forwards trying to determine the route of ley lines, but that could well be a complete waste of time as they could find that they had simply been following the route of an underground stream or water source.

Pendulums may also be used in psychic investigations. A pendulum is a length of cord which is attached to either a small weight constructed from wood or metal or, as is my preference, a small quartz crystal suspended from a light chain approximately seven or eight inches in length. Hold the end of the chain, allowing the pendulum to hang straight down. The pendulum must be completely still. It must then be asked to indicate 'yes' and 'no'. It will respond by either revolving in a clockwise or an anticlockwise direction; it may swing from side to side or backwards and forwards. It is up to each individual to establish the relevant response and its meaning, as these can differ from person to person.

Once you have established the relevant pendulum reactions for 'yes' and 'no', you can ask the pendulum many questions. It can also be used to locate psychically active areas in much the same way as dowsing rods. It will swing or spin more and more rapidly as it comes closer to psychic energy or a spirit presence.

Not all investigators use dowsing rods or pendulums, but they can add an interesting element to paranormal investigations.

## A Tape Recorder

A tape recorder is a definite must, both to record events during séances and to place at strategic points within the location in order to record possible spirit activity. Over the years there have been some very interesting cases of 'electronic voice phenomenon', where people have claimed that they have caught spirit voices on tape.

## Cameras

Cameras are another essential, though the choice of camera is of course a personal preference. There is an argument that people will only capture 'orbs' (the first manifestation of spirit presence), or 'life lights' as I prefer to call them, using a digital camera. I, however, have found this not to be the case. When my wife Gwen has accompanied me on investigations and has taken photographs using both digital and ordinary flash cameras, orbs have been captured with both camera types, together with many other examples of spirit activity.

At least one video camera together with a tripod really is a necessity. This may be placed in a locked-off position in a room in an effort to capture evidence of spirit presence. This may take the form of floating orbs, ectoplasm or, in rare cases, movement of furniture or other items. If two or three video cameras can be positioned in the same room, clearly surveying the whole area, so much the better. Should any movement take place, the fact that it is filmed from all angles can prove that there was no human interference. It is unfortunate that on certain occasions the movement of an object has been captured on film but because only one camera has been used there has always been the argument that 'somebody moved it' – that 'somebody' being a solid and earthly person.

## Man's Best Friend

It has long been stated that man's best friend is his dog. A ghost hunter's best friend can be a dog too!

All animals are psychic. It is not by chance that a pet cat or dog will know exactly when its owner is due to walk through the front door. I have received numerous communications from people telling me that their beloved cat or dog 'always knows' when they are about to arrive home, even though they have not been following a regular pattern of behaviour. Gwen has often told me that she knows that I will be arriving home shortly because the dogs will walk over to the kitchen door and sit there waiting. I too have noticed that should Gwen be away from the home, I can put the kettle on when one of our cats stations himself on the window ledge to peer at the front gate.

Stories abound of animals who have alerted their owners to unseen presences in their homes. There have also been numerous tales of guard dogs refusing to enter certain parts of properties. One such story involves a security guard and his dog who used to regularly patrol St John's Centre in Liverpool. The dog was a large black German Shepherd named Sabre, who was known for his fearlessness when dealing with intruders. However, there was one part of the shopping mall that Sabre refused to visit. He would strain at his lead, bark and growl when encouraged to walk there. It was a spot where an unfortunate accident had taken place during the construction of the centre. A young builder had fallen to his death and his spirit was known to revisit the scene.

It makes perfect sense to me therefore that a dog would be an excellent companion when undertaking the investigation of an allegedly haunted location. Not every dog is afraid, of course. Some dogs may acknowledge a spirit presence by wagging their tail whilst looking towards something that they can see but that you cannot. Others may bark and run up to an area where nothing is discernible to you. Others may display fear, just like Sabre, by refusing to go into or past a certain area. But if you have a dog, take it along! It can only add to the fun and provide a warm furry body to snuggle up to during those long dark vigils.

These are my suggestions for equipment to use when conducting a ghost hunt. Of course if you are technically adept, you will be able to devise your own methods.

These may include buzzers, bells and alarms which will sound if activity is detected, and infra-red rays (similar to the type used in security systems) which will sound an alarm when broken. There are many ingenious devices – the choice is yours. However, with the few simple items I have mentioned, a ghost hunt may be conducted quite satisfactorily.

## Other Preparations

Once you have your kitbag together, there are a few other preparations to make before starting your investigation.

It is always necessary to rule out in advance the more worldly explanations for noises or movements which could in the excitement of the moment be attributed to a ghostly presence. I recall visiting one location where the chandelier was said to swing when 'the spirits' were around. An examination of the alcove in which the chandelier hung showed loose-fitting window panes which allowed quite a strong draught through. Needless to say, 'the spirits' only made their presence felt on breezy days!

Breezes are not the only thing to look out for. Loose floorboards are an extremely common source of 'ghostly' creaks and groans. Water pipes can create some unearthly noises in the wee small hours, especially in older properties. The noise created by a badly fitting door in a draughty old house can have the hairs on your neck standing on end. Even the scurrying of mice in an old house can be mistaken for something less worldly. The branch of a tree persistently tapping on a window or roof can cause the unprepared investigator to assume that they are not alone. The natural cooling down and settlement of a house at night can create a series of noises which sound very much like footsteps ascending and descending a staircase. If a fireplace has been used, the brickwork cooling can make slight creaking and cracking noises. All these eventualities have to be taken into consideration before an investigation can commence.

If you intend using a trigger object – a cross, coin, book, etc. – it should be placed on a sheet of white paper and a pencil outline drawn around its base before the investigation begins. It is preferable to train a video camera or cameras on the object to capture on film any movement that may occur. Make sure that the whole of the sheet of paper is clearly visible so that should any movement take place, it can be proved that nobody has interfered with the item. The room should then be sealed to prevent anybody entering and inadvertently (or purposely – it has been known!) moving the trigger object.

Also in advance of the investigation taking place, a thermometer should be used to determine the naturally occurring cold and warm areas of the location. Older houses commonly had 'cold rooms' where perishable foods would be stored. Also, it may be that a certain room is warmer than the rest of the house because of the hours that the sun shines there. All things have to be taken into consideration.

Lastly, make sure that you have a map of the location so that everybody involved has a clear understanding of how the rooms relate to one another. This will ensure that when people split off into groups to investigate different parts of the location, nobody will be confused as to where they are.

# Haunted
# Scotland

# THE HIGHLANDS, ISLANDS AND CENTRAL SCOTLAND

Scotland is one of my favourite countries. From its craggy peaks to the gentler slopes leading down to the coast, it is breathtaking. It also has a breathtaking past, with stories of enormous feats of courage peppering the pages of history books. It is little wonder that armies quaked in their boots when they faced the prospect of having to fight the 'Ladies from Hell' – those fearsome soldiers of the Queen's Own Highlanders and the Gordon Highlanders.

The Highlands and islands are full of haunting images with macabre stories of the unknown within the castles of old whose pasts recall the memories of battles fought there. It is no faint-hearted ghost hunter who investigates these locations.

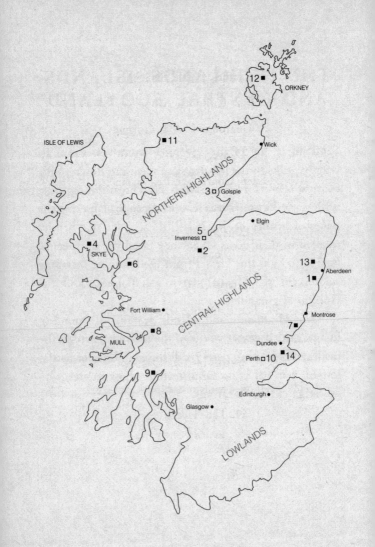

1. Crathes Castle, Banchory

2. Culloden Moor

3. Dunrobin Castle, Golspie

4. Dunvegan Castle, Skye

5. Eden Court Theatre, Inverness

6. Eilean Donan Castle, Loch Duich

7. Ethie Castle, Inverkeilor

8. Glencoe

9. Inverary Castle, Loch Fyne

10. The Salutation Hotel, Perth

11. Sandwood Bay, Sutherland

12. Skaill House, Orkney

13. Swallow Thainstone House, Inverurie

14. The Tay Bridge

# Crathes Castle

Crathes Castle in Aberdeenshire is one of the most popular castles in the care of the National Trust for Scotland. It was built in the second half of the sixteenth century by the Burnetts of Leys. Their first home was on an island in the loch of Leys. The old laird died, leaving a wife and an heir, Alexander. He fell in love with a girl called Bertha, a relative of his who had been left in his mother's care for a few months, but when he returned home from a business trip, he found she had died. Standing by her coffin, full of grief, he reached for a nearby goblet of wine, but his mother quickly snatched it from him and flung it out of the window. Horrified, Alexander realized that she had poisoned Bertha.

Several months later Bertha's father arrived to collect her body. As Lady Agnes and Alexander were talking to him, suddenly the room became very cold and Lady Agnes pointed into thin air, shrieked, 'She comes, she comes!' and fell down dead.

To get away from the scene of all this unhappiness, Alexander left his home and built Crathes Castle.

However, it is said that every year on the anniversary of Bertha's death, a ghost travels from the site of the old castle to Crathes. No one knows whether it is Bertha or Lady Agnes.

Crathes Castle itself is haunted by a Green Lady. She is most frequently seen crossing one of the rooms carrying a baby. When she reaches the fireplace she disappears. She was apparently a young girl who lived at the castle, had an affair with one of the servants and became pregnant. The servant was immediately dismissed and when the girl and her baby disappeared soon afterwards it was rumoured that she had eloped with him. However, not long after that the haunting began, and in the middle of the nineteenth century, when building work was being carried out at the castle, the skeleton of a woman and a baby were found together under a hearthstone. Today the Green Lady is heard more than seen – which is perhaps just as well, as her appearance is said to herald the death of a member of the Burnett family.

---

Crathes Castle, Banchory, AB31 3QJ; Tel: (01330) 844525; Fax: (01330) 844797

Garden and grounds open daily all year; castle open daily 1 April–31 October; restaurant open Wednesday–Sunday 10

January–31 March and 1 November–23 December, daily 1 April–31 October.

The walled garden features yew hedges dating from 1702 and many unusual plants. There are six trails in the grounds and two permanent exhibitions in the visitor centre.

# Culloden Moor

Culloden Moor, to the east of Inverness, was the scene of the last battle fought on British soil. This took place on 16 April 1746 between the Jacobites who supported Bonnie Prince Charlie's claim to the throne and the government forces loyal to the House of Hanover. This was a dynastic struggle which resulted in a civil war, with all the horrors and complexities which that brings. Its roots were steeped in religion and ideology. There were Scots and English on both sides and there were also Highland clansmen among the 8,000 government troops led by the Duke of Cumberland.

The poorly armed and exhausted Jacobite army, which numbered less than 5,000 men, was defeated in under an hour. This effectively settled the fate of the House of Stuart. Over 1,000 men were killed in the battle and many more were slaughtered as they tried to escape afterwards. They were buried on the bleak moorland. Their graves are marked with stones, some bearing the names of their clan. A giant cairn of stones stands as a memorial to the fallen. Bonnie Prince Charlie himself spent five months on the run in the Highlands before he was able to escape to France.

Legend has it that birds do not sing near the graves of the clans and there have been many strange sightings by people crossing Culloden Moor. One evening a party of men were making their way home across the moor when a huge black bird rose from the ground in front of them, blocking out the evening sky. While all stared in shock and disbelief, the apparition disappeared in front of their eyes. It is said that Lord George Murray, the Jacobite commander, had seen a huge black bird on the eve of battle – a bad omen and harbinger of doom. He called it 'a great scree' and in his heart he knew that the next day would not go well for his exhausted and starving men. The last reported sighting of what is called 'the Great Scree of Culloden' was in July 2005.

---

Culloden Battlefield and Visitor Centre, Culloden, Inverness, Highland, IV2 5EU; Tel: (01463) 790607; Fax: (01463) 794294; E-mail: culloden@nts.org.uk

Culloden lies six miles east of Inverness off the B9006. Living History presentations are given at the battlefield throughout the summer.

# Dunrobin Castle

This fairy-tale castle in the north of Scotland is the seat of the Sutherland family. The oldest part dates back to about 1275 but major additions were made at the end of the fourteenth century by Robert, the sixth Earl, who wanted to offer an impressive home to his bride.

During the Jacobite Rebellion the Sutherland family supported the government, and though Dunrobin was captured by the supporters of Bonnie Prince Charlie in 1746, the Earl escaped and managed to retake his castle.

Dunrobin is haunted by Margaret, the daughter of the fourteenth Earl, who lived in the seventeenth century. She fell in love with someone her father considered highly unsuitable and to prevent her from eloping while he arranged a marriage to another suitor, he locked her up in the attic. However, her maid took pity on her, smuggled a rope in and arranged for her lover to wait at the foot of the wall with horses, ready to elope. Unfortunately, just as Margaret was climbing out of the window her father entered the room.

Horrified, she lost her grip and fell to her death. As a result her lover is said to have put a curse on the Earl, while Margaret herself haunts the upper corridors of the castle and can be heard crying for her lost love.

---

Dunrobin Castle, Nr Golspie, Sutherland, KW10 6SF; Tel: (01408) 633268; Fax: (01408) 633268

# Dunvegan Castle

**Dunvegan Castle lies on the eastern shore of Loch Dunvegan to the north-west of the Isle of Skye. It is the ancestral home of the MacLeods and is said to be the oldest inhabited castle in Scotland. Parts date back to the ninth century.**

There are many historic treasures in the castle, including paintings, furniture, books, weapons and trophies. The most famous is the Fairy Flag of the MacLeods. Legend has it that it was given to the clan by a fairy woman who promised to aid the clan in times of need if they waved it. However, it had to be waved no more than three times in total and at intervals of at least a year and a day. So far the flag has been waved twice, both times in battle, once at Glendale in 1490 and once at Trumpan in 1580, and each time it has brought victory to the clan.

The 27th clan chief, Sir Reginald MacLeod, once took the flag to be analysed by the South Kensington Museum. It is apparently made of silk woven in Syria or Rhodes and could have been brought back to Scotland from the Crusades.

People have often heard beautiful music in the room where the flag is kept and ghostly bagpipe music has been heard in the south tower of the castle.

---

Dunvegan Castle, Isle of Skye, IV55 8WF; Tel: (01470) 521206; Fax: (01470) 521205; Website: www.dunvegancastle.com. Open daily except for 25 and 26 December and 1 and 2 January.

# Eden Court Theatre

Eden Court Theatre is the premier arts venue in Inverness, hosting a variety of entertainment, including music, theatre and cinema. It stands on the banks of the Ness, near the cathedral, and was built in the 1970s, but incorporates part of the old Bishop's Palace. Major renovations are currently being carried out, including construction of a second theatre, two new cinemas, two educational studios and a new dressing-room block. The Bishop's Palace will also be renovated and will provide meeting rooms and office accommodation. The theatre will re-open in 2007.

The theatre is haunted by a Green Lady, said to be the wife of one of the bishops who hanged herself there.

The ghost of the murdered King Duncan I has also been seen walking along the banks of the Ness near the theatre. It is not known why he prefers this particular spot.

---

Eden Court, Reay House, Old Edinburgh Road, Inverness, IV3 3HF; Tel: (01463) 239841; Fax: (01463) 713810; Website: www.eden-court.co.uk

# Eilean Donan Castle

**Eilean Donan Castle stands on the edge of Loch Duich in a spectacular setting. It was built in 1260 as a defence against Viking raids and became a base of the MacKenzie family, who installed the MacRae clan as their protectors and the constables of the castle.**

During the Jacobite Rebellion the castle was first a stronghold of government troops, then taken by the Jacobites. In 1719 it was being used as a garrison for Spanish troops and a munitions store when English forces launched a surprise attack with three frigates. The cannon fire set the munitions alight and there was a huge explosion which reduced the castle to ruins. The ghost of a Spanish soldier is said to haunt the castle, but it is not known whether he was killed during that attack or during the nearby Battle of Glenshiel, which took place around the same time.

The castle remained a ruin until it was rebuilt between 1912 and 1932 by Lieutenant Colonel John MacRae-Gilstrap. Today it is one of the most photographed buildings in Scotland and has been used as a location in many films.

Eilean Donan Castle, Dornie, by Kyle of Lochalsh, IV40 8DX; Tel: (01599) 555202; Fax: (01599) 555262; E-mail: info@eilean-donancastle.com; Website: www.eileandonancastle.com. Castle and visitor centre open daily April–October; gift shop open all year.

---

**DEREK'S TIP**

Always thank the spirits after a successful investigation. A little gratitude goes a long way – even in the world beyond.

---

# Ethie Castle

Ethie Castle, near Arbroath, is a fourteenth-century sandstone fortress built by the abbot of Arbroath Abbey. It is said to be Scotland's second oldest permanently inhabited castle.

Probably the best-known person to have lived there was David Beaton, abbot of Arbroath. He moved into the castle in 1524, made many improvements to the property and he and his wife raised their seven children there. He sat in the Scottish parliament from 1525 and in 1539 was appointed Archbishop of St Andrews. He negotiated the marriages of King James V with the French court, but despite his services to the crown he was highly unpopular and on 29 May 1546 was murdered by Protestant reformers at St Andrews. After his death it is said that the monks of Arbroath hid their church vessels, plates and vestments away in the walls of the castle. Not long afterwards Beaton's ghost was seen for the first time at Ethie. He is there still, dragging a gouty leg along the corridors. He is usually seen on a narrow staircase leading to a secret doorway in his former bedroom.

The second ghost at Ethie is that of a child whose remains were found in a hidden room, together with a little wooden cart. He can be heard running across the room and pulling the cart along the floor. He may also be responsible for other strange events in the castle. When the current owners moved in, the pendulum of one of their clocks was broken off in the move and the winder key lost. Nevertheless, the hands of the clock have somehow been moved around to get the chimes to work.

The final ghost at Ethie is a grey lady who walks in the walled garden. Her appearance is said to be a sign that the owner of the house is soon going to die.

---

Ethie Castle, Inverkeilor, by Arbroath, Angus, DD11 5SP; Tel: (01241) 830434; Fax: (01241) 830432; Website: www.ethiecastle.com

# Glencoe

**Probably the most notorious massacre in Scotland took place on 13 February 1692, when a group of government soldiers led by men from the Campbell clan killed the MacIans, a sept of the MacDonalds, in Glencoe, Argyll.**

In August 1691 King William III had offered a pardon to all the Highland clans who had risen against him if they would take an oath of allegiance before 1 January 1692. Alastair MacIan, twelfth chief of Glencoe, not only left it to the last minute to take the oath but also went to the wrong place to do so and therefore missed the deadline. The government was delighted at the opportunity to make an example of the clan and sent two companies of soldiers, about 120 men, to Glencoe, led by Captain Robert Campbell.

Accepting the MacIans' kind offer of hospitality, the soldiers stayed there for several days, but at 5 o'clock in the morning of 13 February, they brutally slaughtered 38 men, women and children of the clan in their beds, including Robert Campbell's niece and her husband. Others died of exposure as they tried to escape across the snowy mountains.

The massacre is said to be re-enacted every year on the anniversary. There have been numerous sightings of it and it has been reported that the screams and cries of the dying ring out across the glen. In Gaelic Glen Coe means 'Valley of Weeping'.

**DEREK'S TIP**

A thermometer is a must for any serious ghost hunter as it will then be possible to detect subtle fluctuations in the temperature of a room.

# Inverary Castle

Inverary Castle, a squat grey turreted mansion on Loch Fyne, is the seat of the Dukes of Argyll. The original Campbell stronghold was burnt by the Marquis of Montrose in 1644 and the present castle was built by the third Duke in 1744. He also rebuilt the nearby town of Inverary at the same time. The castle was subsequently remodelled first by noted architects William and John Adam and then for the second time after a fire in 1877. It houses collections of paintings, tapestries and weapons, including Rob Roy MacGregor's sporran and dirk handle.

The castle is haunted by the Harper of Inverary. According to one story he was hanged by Montrose's men, but according to another he was killed in a castle siege. Either way he has been seen in several parts of the castle, always wearing the Campbell tartan, and his music has often been heard. He seems to be a friendly ghost, but rarely appears to men for some reason.

The castle was also once the scene of a strange vision. On 10 July 1758 Sir William Bart, a doctor, was walking with a friend and a servant in the grounds of the castle when suddenly they all saw a battle taking place in the sky. A Highland regiment was attacking a fort defended by French troops. They were soon beaten back and withdrew, leaving a large number of dead. Later Sir William learned that on that very day a British force of 15,000 men had attacked the French fort of Ticonderoga in Canada and had been forced to retreat, leaving behind 1,994 dead. The 42nd Regiment Black Watch had lost 300 men.

It is said that before the death of each Duke of Argyll a ghostly galley with three men on board, similar to the ship on the Campbells' coat of arms, is seen moving up the loch and then disappearing inland.

---

Inverary Castle, Inverary, Argyll, PA32 8XG; Tel: (01499) 302203. Open Saturday–Thursday April–October, daily July and August.

# The Salutation Hotel

The Salutation Hotel in the centre of the historic city of Perth has been welcoming visitors since 1699 and continues to do so today. The hotel offers modern facilities for conferences and seminars, a banqueting suite for weddings, parties and other special events, a restaurant with traditional Scottish and *à la carte* menus and a bar with a range of beers, wine and spirits, including malt whiskies.

The ghost of Bonnie Prince Charlie himself is said to enjoy the famed hospitality of the hotel. After landing on the Outer Hebridean island of Eriskay in July 1745, he raised his standard at Loch Shiel on 19 August and, after some initial reluctance, several Highland clans joined him in his campaign for the British crown. The Jacobite army marched across Scotland and reached Perth early in September. The prince made the Salutation Hotel his headquarters and the room where he slept is still used as a bedroom. After visiting Scone, where many of his ancestors had been crowned, he moved south to march on London, an ill-fated campaign which eventually came to grief at Culloden *(see page 5)*.

The Salutation Hotel, 34 South Street, Perth, Tayside, PH2 8PH; Tel: (01738) 630066; Fax: (01738) 633598. There is a public car park next to the hotel.

---

## DEREK'S TIP

Try a spot of scrying. Place yourself in front of a mirror in a dimly lit room. Sit quietly and relax into a state of light meditation. You may well find that your features begin to subtly alter to display the face of a person who was known to inhabit the premises under investigation. Obviously do offer up a prayer of protection before attempting such communication and always ensure that you are not alone but have another investigator with you when you attempt this experiment.

# Sandwood Bay

Sandwood Bay is one of the most northerly sandy beaches in Scotland. Backed by huge sand dunes and a loch and flanked by cliffs to the north and Am Buachaille, a magnificent sea stack, to the south, it faces north-west and is a spectacular stretch of coastline.

The bay was said to be a haunt of mermaids until the nineteenth century. It is still reputed to be haunted by the ghost of a sailor who died when a Polish ship went down in the bay. A bearded man wearing sea boots, a sailor's cap and a brass-buttoned tunic has often been seen on the beach.

The nearby Sandwood Loch and ruined Sandwood Cottage are said to be haunted by the ghost of an Australian who used to visit the area. His heavy footsteps can still be heard. The cottage has also been the scene of other strange phenomena. One couple who spent the night there woke to find the ruins shaking and heard the sound of a wild horse stamping on them.

Sandwood Bay, Nr Cape Wrath, Sutherland. The nearest approach by public road is at Blairmore, a few miles north-west of Kinlochbervie. There is a car park there. Go through the gate opposite. The track to Sandwood Bay is four miles long and well signposted.

# Skaill House

**Skaill House is a large mansion lying close to the shore
not far from Skara Brae on Orkney. It was built on the
site of a Pictish burial ground, which may have something to do with the many ghost stories associated with
the house. Visitors and residents alike have reported
strange experiences, including ghostly footsteps and
unseen people sitting down on beds.**

According to one story, a man called Ubby constructed
a little island in the middle of the nearby Skaill Loch by
repeatedly rowing out into the loch and dumping stones
overboard. Eventually he died on the island and legend
has it that his ghost came to Skaill House and has haunted it ever since.

Though many paranormal phenomena have been
reported at the house, there has only been one actual
sighting of a ghost there. Early one morning the clean-
ers were in the courtyard when one of them looked up
and saw a woman with a shawl over her head standing
at the door to one of the apartments. They assumed that
the people staying there were still there and left, think-
ing that they would clean that apartment later. But the

guests had already left and the building had been empty at the time.

---

Skaill House, Breckness Estate, Sandwick, Orkney, KW16 3LR; Tel: (01856) 841815; Fax: (01856) 841885

---

**DEREK'S TIP**

You do not have to limit your investigation to the interior of a building. There are numerous places outdoors where spirit activity has been noted or ghost sightings have been reported. Ancient battlefields or sites where villages and houses once stood are just as likely to render up paranormal activity.

# Swallow Thainstone House

During my last theatre tour, whilst appearing in Aberdeen I stayed at the Swallow Thainstone House hotel. As we arrived at the hotel it was snowing heavily. The old house looked beautiful under its blanket of snow. As we were welcomed in to the hotel and were shown up to our rooms I was psychically aware of the warmth of the atmosphere. I knew nothing of the history of the building, but it was obvious to me that at one time it had been the home of some rather wealthy people.

That night, after the show, I retired to bed, but in the early hours of the morning I was awoken by movement around the bedroom. I could see clairvoyantly that there was the spirit of a young woman dressed in a very old-fashioned riding habit standing by the window of the room looking out over the snow-covered gardens. She stood gazing wistfully out and then started to move back across the room. As she reached the centre she gradually faded from my sight before disappearing completely.

The following morning I was sitting on my own having coffee in the downstairs lounge. The manageress walked in and stopped to have a chat with me. She asked me whether I had sensed anything in the hotel. 'It's haunted, you know, Derek,' she said. She proceeded to tell me the story of a terrible riding accident that had taken place in the grounds. The daughter of the family who once lived there had been out riding when her horse stumbled and fell, crushing her beneath its weight. She passed to spirit in the house as a result of her injuries.

'Ah! So that's who paid me a visit last night,' I said. 'And I suppose that the room I'm staying in was once her bedroom?'

'Well, we just couldn't resist it now, could we?' she replied, laughing.

---

Swallow Thainstone House, Inverurie, Grampian, AB51 5NT; Tel: (01467) 621643

# The Tay Bridge

The first railway bridge over the River Tay in Dundee, designed by Thomas Bouch, opened on 26 September 1877. It had taken 6 years to build and 10 million bricks, 2 million rivets, 87,000 cubic feet of timber and 15,000 casks of cement. Queen Victoria crossed it in the summer of 1879 and knighted Bouch soon afterwards.

Everything went well at first, but on 28 December 1879 there was a storm so fierce that the engineers were worried that the structure would be weakened. They tried to alert the railway authorities to the danger, but it was too late and a train had already started to cross the bridge. It collapsed under the weight and the train plunged into the river. Seventy-nine people were killed.

Speculation is still rife concerning the exact cause of the disaster, but it brought about a countrywide review of bridge safety. Thomas Bouch died shortly afterwards, a broken man. A new, modified Tay Bridge was built parallel to the original bridge in 1885, using the orignal undamaged girders. Many people claim to have seen a ghost train at the site of the old bridge on the anniversary of the disaster and to have heard people screaming.

# THE LOWLANDS

And so to the Lowlands and the gentler Scottish land-scape – but there is nothing gentle in the history of this part of the country. From the Ayrshire coast to Glasgow and on to Edinburgh where the Devil is said to have walked, the paranormal investigator will be spoiled for choice as far as locations for a ghost hunt are concerned.

The most fascinating locations that I have investi-gated in this area of the country have been the exten-sive vaults which lie beneath the Old Town of Edinburgh. All manner of paranormal activity is to be experienced here – and don't forget that it was in this place that the infamous body snatchers Burke and Hare plied their trade.

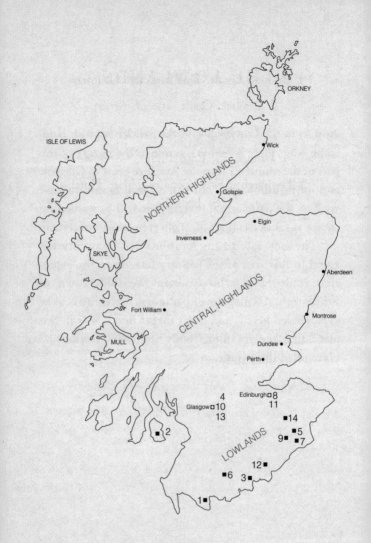

1. Baldoon Castle, Dumfries and Galloway

2. Brodick Castle, Isle of Arran

3. Comlongon Castle, Dumfries

4. Dalmarnock Road Bridge, Glasgow

5. Dryburgh Abbey Country House Hotel,
   St Boswells

6. The Globe Inn, Dumfries

7. Jedburgh Castle Jail and Museum

8. The Last Drop Tavern, Edinburgh

9. Melrose Abbey

10. The Pavilion Theatre, Glasgow

11. The Royal Mile, Edinburgh

12. Spedlin's Tower, Dumfries and Galloway

13. The Theatre Royal, Glasgow

14. Thirlestane Castle, Lauder

# Baldoon Castle

Baldoon Castle in Bladnoch, not far from Wigtown, was built in the early sixteenth century. It was owned by the Dunbars of Westfield from 1530 to 1800, but is now a ruin.

In the mid-seventeenth century the castle was owned by Sir David Dunbar. His son and heir was also called David and it was arranged that he would marry Janet, the eldest daughter of Sir James Dalrymple, a local landowner. She was in love with Archibald, third Lord Rutherford, but as he was practically penniless, her parents persuaded her to marry David instead. They were married in the kirk of Old Luce, two miles from Carsecleugh Castle, the home of the Dalrymples.

On the wedding night, however, the servants were alarmed by hideous screaming coming from the bridal chamber. When they finally broke the door down they found the bridegroom lying across the threshold, badly wounded and covered in blood, and Janet, also covered in blood, cowering in a corner. She never recovered her senses and died insane a few weeks later, on 12 September 1669. Her husband survived, but would never talk about what had happened.

There are several theories as to what had taken place. Some people think Janet attacked her bridegroom, while others think that he attacked her and she stabbed him in self-defence. Another theory is that Archibald hid in the room, attacked David and then escaped through the window. According to local legend, the Devil himself did it.

David later married a daughter of the seventh Earl of Eglinton and died in 1682 after falling off his horse. Archibald never married and died in 1685. Sir Walter Scott used the story in his novel *The Bride of Lammermuir*.

Every year on the anniversary of her death Janet's ghost wanders the ruins of the castle, still screaming and covered in blood.

---

Baldoon Castle, Bladnoch, Nr Wigtown, Wigtownshire, Dumfries and Galloway

# Brodick Castle

Brodick Castle stands at the foot of Goatfell mountain, two miles north of Brodick, the main port on the Isle of Arran. The name Brodick comes from the Norse for 'broad bay'. The place on which the castle now stands may have been the site of a Viking fort. Parts of the castle date back to the thirteenth century, though most of the original castle, built by the Stewarts, was destroyed in 1406 by the English. The first Duke of Hamilton was executed by Oliver Cromwell in the mid-seventeenth century and Cromwell placed a garrison of 80 soldiers in the castle. They restored part of it and later, in the nineteenth century, it was extensively renovated.

The older part of the castle is said to be haunted by a Grey Lady. She is said to be the ghost of a Cromwellian servant girl. The captain of the guard had an affair with her and when she was found to be expecting his child, she was dismissed from service at the castle. Her family lived at Corrie, just a few miles from Brodick. When they heard of her plight they disowned their daughter. She drowned herself in the sea at the Wine Port, a red sandstone quay at the entrance to Brodick

Castle. Her ghost haunts the lower corridor, kitchen and turnpike stairs which lead to the East Tower and battlements. She has been seen standing over staff scrubbing floors, as if in conversation with them, but the workers never see her.

Another ghost, that of a man, has appeared in the library, and it is said that a white hart is seen in the grounds of the castle whenever the clan chief of the Hamiltons is about to die.

---

Brodick Castle, Brodick, Isle of Arran, KA27 8HY; Tel: (01770) 302202; Fax: (01770) 302312; E-mail: Website: brodick-castle@nts.org.uk

The castle is open daily April–October. The gardens and country park are open daily all year round. There is a licensed restaurant and souvenir shop and the castle may be hired for weddings and other functions.

# Comlongon Castle

**Comlongon Castle in Dumfries dates back to the fifteenth century and stands in over 120 acres of gardens, parkland and woodland just a few minutes from the Scottish–English border. The original tower house is attached to a later mansion, which is now a privately run family hotel renowned as the perfect location for a wedding.**

The castle itself dates from the fifteenth century and was built by the Murray family of Cockpool. The tower house is a well-preserved border fortress of pink dressed sandstone. Guests can take a candlelit tour of the medieval keep and Great Hall, which was used as a living and banqueting room. Unusually, the castle has retained its hinged iron gate, or yett, a defensive feature which was placed immediately behind the studded oak door. The borders were a wild place in the past, with endemic feuding, raiding and kidnapping, and in 1606 the Privy Council ordered the destruction of all the yetts there in an effort to bring peace to the area.

Another unusual feature of the castle is the mummified cats which were discovered during a recent excavation of the basement. It is thought that they were sealed up alive when the castle was built in order to protect it from evil spirits. They are now on display in the basement.

The ghost who haunts the castle is said to be Lady Marion Carruthers, who lived in the mid-sixteenth century. She was the daughter of Sir Simon Carruthers, Baron of Mouswald Castle, four miles from Comlongon, and on his death she and her sister Janet inherited his estate. Two powerful local families, the Douglases of Drumlanrigh and the Maxwells of Caerlaverock Castle, hoped to get their hands on it, however, and Sir James Douglas had obtained Sir Simon's consent to marry Marion. In order to stake his claim instead, Lord Maxwell took the castle by force and occupied it. The case was settled in James's favour by the Privy Council in 1563, but Marion fled to her uncle, Sir William Murray, at Comlongon Castle and gave him half her dowry in an attempt to avoid the marriage. However, James sued for his 'just inheritance' and again won the case. At that point, on 25 September 1570, Lady Marion threw herself from the lookout tower of Comlongon Castle. Later it was rumoured that this was not suicide, as was first thought, but murder by some of James's men, who had thrown her from the battlements so that their master would gain the estate without having to marry such a reluctant bride.

No grass would grow on the spot where Lady Marion fell and since then there have been many strange phenomena at the castle and the ghostly figure of a young lady has been seen wandering about in tears.

---

Comlongon Castle, Clarencefield, Dumfries, DG1 4NA; Tel: (01387) 870283; Fax: (01387) 870266; E-mail: reception@comlongon.co.uk; Website: www.comlongon.co.uk

# Dalmarnock Road Bridge

**Dalmarnock Road Bridge is one of the eight bridges over the River Clyde in central Glasgow. It is the most easterly of the bridges and joins Dalmarnock on the north side of the river and Rutherglen on the south.**

Originally there was a ford at Dalmarnock, then in 1821 a timber pay bridge was built. Another timber bridge replaced it in 1848. Dalmarnock had become a district of Glasgow in 1846. The present bridge was built in 1891 by the engineers Crouch and Hogg and was the first bridge over the Clyde to have a flat road surface. It comprises five elegant spans supported by concrete-filled wrought-iron cylinders. It was refurbished in 1997, but many of the original Gothic parapets were retained.

The bridge is haunted by the ghost of a man who committed suicide there. He seems to be a solid and normal-looking man about 30 years old with short hair, wearing a navy three-quarter length coat and black trousers. As he stands on the bridge, staring into the Clyde, people have mistaken him for a real person who is about to commit suicide. But then he jumps off the bridge and vanishes into thin air.

# Dryburgh Abbey Country House Hotel

**Dryburgh Abbey Country House Hotel is situated in 10 acres of grounds on the banks of the Tweed next to the atmospheric ruins of the twelfth-century Dryburgh Abbey. It was built in the mid-nineteenth century on the site of a previous house.**

A woman living in the former house in the sixteenth century fell in love with a monk from the abbey – or some say it was a clergyman – and they started an affair. For a while they managed to keep it secret, but then the abbot learned of it and had the monk sentenced to death for breaking his vows. He was hanged in full view of the house. Grief-stricken, the woman threw herself over the bridge into the Tweed and drowned. Her ghost is said to appear on the bridge and sometimes in the hotel as well, especially when renovations are being carried out. She is known as the Grey Lady.

The abbey ruins are reputed to be haunted by many monks, and the sound of plainchant has been heard there on several occasions. Sir Walter Scott and Field Marshal Haig are buried there.

Dryburgh Abbey Country House Hotel, St Boswells, Melrose, TD6 0RQ; Tel: (01835) 822261; Fax: (01835) 823945; E-mail: enquiries@dryburgh.co.uk; Website: www.dryburgh.co.uk

**DEREK'S TIP**

If using an EMF meter in your investigation, attempt to locate any electrical wiring or equipment on the premises you have chosen, as these will adversely affect the readings of such meters.

# The Globe Inn

The Globe Inn in Dumfries was established in 1610 and is known for its association with Robert Burns, the national poet of Scotland. The first Burns Supper was held there in 1819. Burns called the inn a place where he enjoyed 'many a merry squeeze', and some of these were with a barmaid, Anna Park. She gave birth to a daughter called Elizabeth, but died soon afterwards. Burns never denied that he was the father and he and his wife raised the child as their own. Burns' favourite seat is still in the inn and the poetry that he etched on his bedroom windows with a diamond can still be seen.

Some say that Anna Park can still be seen too. The inn is definitely haunted by an eighteenth-century barmaid, though it is not certain that she is Anna. However, she is very friendly and appears whenever there are changes at the inn or when the bar is full of laughter. She has a sense of mischief and is said to move things around just for fun and to tug at people's sleeves to get their attention.

There have also been sightings of a White Lady in the pub, especially at Burns Suppers.

The Globe Inn, 56 High Street, Dumfries, Dumfries and Galloway, DG1 2JA; Tel: (01387) 252335; Website: www.globeinndumfries.co.uk

---

**DEREK'S TIP**

When researching a location, attempt to establish the local dialect or language of a particular spirit reputed to haunt the building. Calling out using that dialect or language may encourage a response from the spirit person or people.

# Jedburgh Castle Jail and Museum

Jedburgh Castle Jail was built as a Howard reform prison in 1823 on the site of Jethart Castle, which was demolished in 1409 to keep it out of the hands of the English. It is the only one of its kind left in Scotland. Men, women and children were held there, but it was mainly used for debtors. It was notorious for its cruelty and terrible conditions and was finally closed in 1886 after larger prisons were built in Edinburgh and Glasgow and all the prisoners were transferred. The women's and children's cell blocks are now open to the public and part of the building has been converted into a museum of social history featuring exhibitions of nineteenth-century prison life.

Several visitors to the jail have felt that unseen people were there with them. Some have heard footsteps and cell doors banging and seen unusual lights. A team of paranormal investigators from the Glamorgan Paranormal Society investigated the property recently and recorded orbs of light, flashing lights, smoke, people whistling, doors creaking and the sound of something brushing against the cell walls. Most of them heard ghostly footsteps slowly walking along a corridor.

Jedburgh Castle Jail and Museum, Castlegate, Jedburgh, TD8 6QD; Tel: (01835) 86254; Fax: (01835) 864750; E-mail: museums@scotborders.gov.uk; Website: www.scotborders.gov.uk/outabout/museums/3249.html. Open 21 Mar–31 Oct.

---

**DEREK'S TIP**

Remember that spirits do not always appear at night. They are just as likely to be in visitation during daylight hours. It is, however, far more atmospheric to conduct an investigation during the hours of darkness.

---

# The Last Drop Tavern

The Last Drop Tavern is a traditional pub in Edinburgh's Grassmarket, where the city's public hangings used to take place. The name refers both to the last hanging there, in the eighteenth century, and to the drop through which the prisoner fell. The place where the gallows stood, just opposite the pub, is now marked by a St Andrew's Cross in rose-coloured cobblestones and a plaque with the inscription: 'For the Protestant faith, on this spot many martyrs and covenanters died.'

Originally two tenement buildings stood on the site of the present-day pub, but they were demolished and rebuilt in 1929–30, using the original stone. The door-piece is dated 1634. The use of the old materials may explain the presence of the ghost who haunts the pub – a little girl in medieval clothing. She has often been seen in the cellar and the bar and likes to play tricks on the staff, calling their names when they are alone in the pub.

The Last Drop offers a fine selection of malt whisky as well as traditional food and drink. Rumour has it that the phrase 'one for the road' comes from tradition of giving condemned prisoners their last meal in a pub on the road to the gallows.

---

The Last Drop Tavern, 74–78 Grassmarket, Edinburgh, EH1 2JR; Tel: 0131 225 4851

**DEREK'S TIP**

I would advise that unless you have a trained medium with you, you should not attempt to invoke spirits by using ouija boards or any similar device, especially if the location is reputed to harbour a particularly nasty spirit.

# Melrose Abbey

Melrose Abbey was founded around 1136 by David I and dedicated to the Virgin Mary. It was a Cistercian abbey and became one of the richest in Scotland, with the largest flock of sheep of any of the religious houses in the country – about 15,000 by 1370. The wool was sold as far away as Italy. The abbey was also a centre of learning and politics. It was almost completely demolished by the English in 1385 but was subsequently rebuilt. In the following years, however, it was sacked four times and in 1545 the Earl of Hertford bombarded it with cannon. After that it never regained its previous glory. After the Reformation the monks were not allowed to recruit new members and the community died out in the early 1590s. From 1618 to the nineteenth century part of the nave was used as parish church, but the rest of the abbey was used as a source of building material for the town and cattle and sheep grazed among the ruins.

The heart of Robert the Bruce is buried in the abbey grounds in a leaden casket. He had sponsored the rebuilding of the abbey after an attack by the English in 1322. On 24 June 1998, the anniversary of Bruce's victory over the English at Bannockburn in 1314, the then Scottish Secretary of State, Donald Dewar, unveiled a plinth over the place where the heart is now buried.

Melrose Abbey is said to be haunted by several ghosts, including a group of monks. Michael Scott, a man who is supposed to have practised the black arts, is said to haunt his own grave. A strange figure has also been seen sliding along the ground.

---

Melrose Abbey, Melrose, TD6 9LG; Tel: (01896) 822562. Open daily.

# The Pavilion Theatre

Glasgow's Pavilion Theatre of Varieties opened on 29 February 1904 and is still providing variety today. It seats 1,800 in grand style, with a domed ceiling, rococo plasterwork, Louis XV style decoration, mahogany woodwork and a marble mosaic floor.

All the most famous stars of the music hall played at the Pavilion and it is said that some are still there. The comedian Tommy Morgan was a big hit in the mid-twentieth century and when he died in 1961 his ashes were scattered on the roof of the theatre. His ghost is said to wander the upper floor and backstage areas.

A ghostly woman has also been sighted in one of the boxes in the auditorium and a phantom pianist occasionally plays on stage. There may also be a few spectral stagehands about, as most of the theatre staff have had the disconcerting experience of finding items of equipment moved around or even having them disappear from right under their noses!

The Pavilion Theatre, 121 Renfield Street, Glasgow, G2 3AX; Tel:
0141 332 1846 (box office); Website:www.paviliontheatre.co.uk

---

**DEREK'S TIP**

If you decide to form a circle in order to generate energy to assist spirit people in drawing close, ensure you maintain physical contact with the people who are sitting or standing on either side of you. This is important, as if contact is broken, the energy is diminished.

---

# The Royal Mile, Edinburgh

Edinburgh's Royal Mile runs from Edinburgh Castle to the gates of Holyrood House and is one of the oldest parts of the city. Daniel Defoe called the 'Largest, Longest and Finest Street in the World', though it actually consists of several connected streets: Castlehill, Lawnmarket, High Street, Canongate and Abbey Street.

At one end of the Royal Mile the ancient Edinburgh Castle stands proudly on the site of a former volcano, while at the other end Scotland's new parliament building is situated in front of the spectacular Holyrood Park and Salisbury Crags. In between there are numerous historic buildings of interest, including the Free Church of Scotland New College and Assembly Hall and St Giles' Cathedral. Holyrood House itself was built in the early sixteenth century by James IV and is now Queen Elizabeth II's official residence in Scotland.

Legend has it that the Royal Mile is haunted by a death coach. The death coach, *cóiste bodhar*, *coach-a-baur* or hellwain appears in many traditions, especially those of Ireland and the Isle of Man. It may simply come to claim the souls of people who have just died, or it may race through towns and villages at dead of night, picking up unwary souls and carrying them away to hell.

In Edinburgh, the death coach travels along the Royal Mile from Holyrood House to the castle, drawn by a team of black horses. Some say they are headless, while others say they have flashing eyes and breathe fire. According to Edinburgh tradition, if the death coach is sighted, there will be a disaster in the city.

# Spedlin's Tower

Spedlin's Tower stands by the River Annan, four miles north-west of Lockerbie. It was built around 1500 and was a stronghold of the Jardines of Applegarth. In the nineteenth century they built a new mansion, Jardine Hall, nearby and the tower fell into decay. It was restored first in the 1960s and then again in 1988–9.

In the 1650s Sir Alexander Jardine imprisoned a miller, Dunty Porteus, for making bad bread, then left shortly afterwards for Edinburgh with the dungeon keys in his pocket. It was some months before anyone remembered the prisoner was there and in the meantime he had died of starvation. When he was found it was discovered that in a desperate attempt to reach the door he had literally torn his hands from the manacles which bound him to the wall – or had possibly even eaten them away. For years afterwards his ghost could be heard screaming with hunger and pain. Finally, in an effort to lay it to rest, the family had a Bible built into the wall of the dungeon. This gradually started to decay and in 1710 was sent to Edinburgh to be rebound. Immediately the screaming broke out again and a series of catastrophes befell the family. Once the Bible was put back into the dungeon, peace was restored.

Some say the ghost moved with the Jardine family to their new mansion in the nineteenth century. Others, however, have heard strange moans in the tower and felt that a mysterious presence was watching them. Some claim to have actually seen a tall white-haired apparition around the site of the dungeon. He looks distraught and has no hands.

According to local tradition, if you poke a stick into the dungeon of Spedlin's Tower it will come back half-chewed.

---

Spedlin's Tower, Templand, Dumfries and Galloway

# The Theatre Royal, Glasgow

The Theatre Royal, Glasgow, first opened in 1867, but two fires swept the building and it had to close while restoration work was carried out. It reopened in September 1895 and since that time has presented a wide variety of drama, dance, comedy, opera and musical theatre. At one time it was used by Scottish Television to record *The One O'Clock Gang* and it is now home to the Scottish Opera and Scottish Ballet companies and is also available for conferences, meetings and seminars.

The theatre is said to be haunted by at least two ghosts. One is Nora, a cleaner who aspired to be an actress but wasn't taken seriously. In despair she threw herself off the upper circle. Now her ghost can be heard moaning and slamming doors.

The second ghost appears in the sub-basement. Tradition has it that he is a fireman who drowned there while on duty in the 1960s. He has also been seen in the orchestra pit.

The Theatre Royal, 282 Hope Street, Glasgow, G2 3QA; Tel: 0141 240 1133 (box office); Website: www.theatreroyalglasgow.com

There is a fully-licensed restaurant and café. Function rooms are available for corporate events.

---

**DEREK'S TIP**

If you are tempted to try to invoke spirit people without the presence of a trained medium, do ensure that you offer up a prayer of self-protection first.

# Thirlestane Castle

Thirlestane Castle, at Lauder, in the Border hills, is one of the oldest castles in Scotland. It was originally a thirteenth-century defensive fort and was rebuilt by the Maitland family in the sixteenth century. At the time of the Civil War they supported King Charles I and the second Earl of Lauderdale was imprisoned for nine years in the Tower of London as a result. On the Restoration of the monarchy in 1660, he became Secretary of State for Scotland and effectively ruled Scotland as a member of King Charles II's Cabal Cabinet (the 'l' of 'cabal' stood for Lauderdale). His ghost is said to haunt the castle and grounds.

Recently it has also been claimed that there is a haunted corridor in the castle. It is said that people who walk down it never return.

---

Thirlestane Castle, Lauder, Berwickshire, TD2 6RU; Tel: (01578) 722430; Fax: (01578) 722761; E-mail: admin@thirlestanecastle.co.uk; Website: www.thirlestanecastle.co.uk. Open Easter–October.

The castle is situated just off the A68 going into Lauder. There is a tea room, gift shop, picnic area and children's adventure playground and several woodland walks.

## DEREK'S TIP

If your group is planning to split up in order to conduct lone vigils, do make sure that everybody is equipped with some form of communication, i.e. walkie-talkie or mobile phone, and do make sure that as many people as possible carry a camera of sorts.

# INDEX OF PLACES

# HAUNTED BRITAIN

## DEREK ACORAH

Out now in all good bookstores is the **unabridged** edition of Derek Acorah's *Haunted Britain*. In this fascinating guide, Derek Acorah explores over 100 haunted sites throughout Great Britain, ranging from haunted castles and manors to shopping centres, hotels, beaches and even bowling alleys. Organized by geographical area, *Haunted Britain* is an ideal travelling companion, or simply offers the perfect read. Each section provides helpful information on opening hours and access.

Coming soon…

# HAUNTED BRITAIN AND IRELAND

## DEREK ACORAH

Publishing in December 2006, this expanded edition of *Haunted Britain* includes a new section on the Republic of Ireland.